Quotations
To
Tickle Your Brain

Lindsay Collier

"Be what you is not what you ain't. Cause if you is what you ain't, you ain't what you is"

Ten reasons why you need this book

1. It's quick and easy to read.

2. By using these quotes people will think you are smarter than you are.

3. It cost much less than a shrimp cocktail.

4. It has less fat than a shrimp cocktail.

5. It'll change the way you think- forever.

6. You'll have a lot of fun reading it.

7. You can give it to your boss and suggest s/he may want to take a few cues from it.

8. You'll never run out of things to say again.

9. It'll make you laugh and feel good.

10. I could use the money.

About the Author

Lindsay Collier has been at the leading edge of creativity in organizations for more than 30 years.. A former creativity expert and futurist at Kodak, he emerged as a major influence in helping many organizations create breakthrough futures. He has a unique combination of material that includes state of the art creative and future thinking techniques, combined with a few dashes of humor for taking people to places they've never been.

Author of several books and a popular keynote speaker Lindsay is now semi retired and living in The Villages, Florida. His current project is to build a library of books and EBooks based on his years of experience on helping people expand their creative thinking capacity.

He can be reached at lindsaycollier@comcast.net or via his Facebook or Linkedin sites.

Introduction

Quotations are great tools for helping people change the way they think. I use them constantly in my presentations and workshops and have been collecting them for years. Here's my chance to share my favorites with you, and you're going to love them - guaranteed!. These particular quotations have one thing in common - they all relate to thinking more creatively. Each one has the capacity to challenge you in some aspect of your thinking.

You may want to use these for your own personal growth or in a group, team, or family setting. The question to ask is, "What is the essence of this quotation and in what ways does it shape my current thinking?" Have fun with each one and let them really challenge you.

There are a few of these that have lost their owners and I feel bad about that. If you know the source of some of the anonymous ones, please let me know. I feel strongly about crediting the originators and have done this whenever possible. These quotations represent the collective advice of several hundred people and I wish I knew who all these people were. I'd love to be able to invite them all over my house for an evening's worth of great conversation.

I'd also be interested in any favorites you might want to share with me. Oh, by the way, there are a few of my originals thrown in too.

Here's a few ways you might use these. Better still, make up your own ways, and let me know about them.

- Post them in the wall of conference meetings prior to meeting.
- Put them on index cards and use as a warm-up exercise before a workshop.
- Pick them randomly at meetings to supply thought excursions.
- Use as homework between sessions.
- Use to generate a group motto or song.

- Make a customized quotation based on the essence of one that sounds interesting.
- Make them silly.
- Have people tape them to their foreheads or shirts and use in an introductory exercise.
- Write short essays expanding their meaning.
- Pick one each day that you will use to guide you through the rough spots.
- Treat them like baseball cards and trade them with your friends.
- Stick a new one on the visor of your car everyday for the ride to work.
- Leave carefully chosen ones on the walls of your associates or boss to drop hints.
- Tape one under each chair before a meeting and have people read them.
- Use one in your email signature and change it often
- Pass them out to strangers who look like they could use a real boost.
- Stick some on local bulletin boards.
- Use some as a screen saver on your computer.

On the road to the future there are drivers,
passengers, and road kill.

C. K. Prahalad

Every great oak was once a nut
that stood its ground.

Anonymous

The real happy person is the one who can enjoy
the scenery on a detour.

Anonymous

All great accomplishments were once considered
impossible.

Fortune Cookie

You miss 100% of the shots you don't take.

Wayne Gretsky

Think left and think right and think low and think high. Oh the thinks you can think up if only you try.

Dr. Seuss

A bird does not sing because it has an answer. It sings because it has a song.

Yorok Indian

A new idea is first condemned as ridiculous and then dismissed as trivial, until it finally becomes what everyone knows.

William Jones

Be the change you are trying to create.

Gandhi

No problem can stand the assault of sustained thinking.

Voltaire

If you think you're too small to be significant then you've never been in bed with a mosquito.

Bette Reese

In times of profound change, the learners inherit the earth, while the learned find themselves beautifully equipped to deal with a world that no longer exists.

Al Rogers

The factory of the future will have only two employees, a man and a dog. The man will be there to feed the dog. The dog will be there to keep the man from touching the equipment.

Warren Bennis

The worst part about being in the rat race is that, even if you win, you're still a rat.

We're all in this alone.

Lily Tomlin

Our greatest weakness lies in giving up. The most certain way to succeed is always to try just one more time.

My principle interest is in giving commercial progress to the misdirected ideas of others.

Thomas Edison

Angels can fly because they take themselves lightly.

Anonymous

Anyone who's ever taken a shower has had a good idea.

Nolan Bushnell

He who wants milk should not stand in the middle of a pasture and wait for a cow to back up to him.

Anonymous

No one tests the depth of a river with both feet.

An African proverb

It's what you learn after you know it all that counts.

John Wooden

Creativity is thinking up new things. Innovation is doing new things.

Theodore Levitt

There ain't no rules around here. We're trying to accomplish something.

Thomas Edison

Business's three worst enemies are thinking too big, thinking too small, and thinking too much.

Anonymous

An inventor is simply a person who doesn't take their education too seriously.

Charles Kettering

Where the light is the brightest the shadows are the deepest.

Wolfgang Goethe

Change favors the prepared mind.

Louis Pasteur

Get your facts first. Then you can distort them as much as you please.

Mark Twain

Ideas are like children. They're really cute when they're your own.

Anonymous

The test of a first rate intelligence is the ability to hold two opposing ideas in the mind at the same time and still retain the ability to function.

F. Scott Fitzgerald

Faced with the choice between changing one's mind and proving there is no need to do so, most people get busy on the proof.

J.K. Galbraith

The biggest mistake that you'll ever make in your life is to believe that you work for somebody else.

Earl Nightingale

A failure is a person who has blundered, but is not able to cash in on the experience.

Elbert Hubbard

The higher you climb the flagpole, the more people see your rear end.

Don Meridith

The ability to convert visions to things is the secret of success.

Henry Ward Beecher

Everything in the universe is programmed to grow. You can change without growing but you can't grow without changing.

Larry Wilson

There is no reason why a kaleidoscope should not have as much fun as a telescope.

Mark Twain

Organizational change is like dancing with a gorilla. You don't stop when you get tired; you stop when the gorilla gets tired.

Anonymous

A cow chip is a picnic to a fly.

Texas Bix Bender

The future is a lot like the present, only shorter.

Goose Gossage

15

The definition of insanity is when you keep doing the same thing over and over again, each time hoping for different results.

Edward Deming

No snowflake ever falls in the wrong place.

Zen

When I examine myself and my methods of thought, I come to the conclusion that the gift of fantasy has meant more to me than my talent for absorbing positive knowledge.

Albert Einstein

Every exit is an entry somewhere else.

Tom Stoppard

What we need is more people who specialize in the impossible.

Theodore Roethke

It's never too late to have a happy childhood. You are only young once, but you can be immature all your life.

Anonymous

Nothing is more imprecise than precision.

Eugene Ionesco

The best way to destroy your enemy is to make him your friend.

Abraham Lincoln

17

*We can't all be heroes. Someone has to sit on the
curb and clap as they go by.*

Will Rogers

*If we think small we'll become big. But if we think
like we're big we'll grow small.*

Herb Kelleher

*The desk is a dangerous place from which to
observe the world.*

John LeCarre

*Better to move forward and stumble than to stand
still and grumble.*

Teresa Miller

How old would you be if you didn't know how old you were?

Satchel Page

Ideas are like belly buttons; everyone has one.

John Janning

If the roof doesn't leak then the architect hasn't been creative enough.

Frank Lloyd Wright

Verbal diarrhea is created by people who make vowel movements consonantly.

Anonymous

From a hayloft, a horse looks like a violin.

Lord Chesterfield

*That which has been believed by everyone, always
and everywhere, has every chance of being false.*

Paul Valery

Seek simplicity - then distrust it.

Alfred North Whithead

The shell must break before the bird can fly.

Lord Tennyson Alfred

*If we think more about failing at what we are
doing than about doing it, we will not succeed.*

Warren Bennis

Never play leap frog with a bull.

Texas Bix Bender

One of the most critical abilities you have is the ability to close your mind.

David Zach

In most organizations, the future doesn't have a lobbying group.

Fortune Magazine

We need to help people to do what they would have done if they had known they could have done it.

Dan Burrus

Optimists see an opportunity in every problem. Pessimists see a problem in every opportunity.

Anonymous

If you have a garden and a library, you have everything you need.

ICicero

The surest way to go broke is to sit around waiting for a break.

Anonymous

Exhilaration is that feeling just after a great idea hits you and before you realize what's wrong with it.

Bernard Meltzer

The things that got you to where you are today are not the things that will get you to the future.

Peter Drucker

Be what you is, not what you ain't - cause if you is what you ain't, you ain't what you is.

Luther Price

No snowflake in an avalanche feels responsible.

Anonymous

There is no right way to do the wrong thing.

Anonymous

Intelligent people, when assembled into an organization, will tend toward collective stupidity.

Karl Albrecht

Only mediocre people are always at their best.

Somerset Magham

A vision without a task is but a dream. A task without a vision is drudgery. A vision and a task is the hope of the world.

A church in Sussex, England, 1730

Just cause everything is changed doesn't mean anything is different.

Alfred E. Neuman

An old error is always more popular than a new truth.

German Proverb

He who lives in a pool of crocodiles long enough grows a snout just like one of them.

Zulu saying

Don't be afraid to take a big step if it's needed.
You can't cross a chasm in two small leaps.

Anonymous

Many a man fails as an original thinker simply
because his memory is too good.

Nietzsche

A crank is a man with a new idea - until it catches
on.

Mark Twain

Great teams flourish only when individuals have a
shot at stardom.

Mike Vance

25

Life is a run-on sentence. The object is to punctuate it with experience.

William Finegan

I don't want any yes men around me. I want people who will tell me the truth even if it means their job.

Samuel Goldwyn

I'd give my right arm to be ambidextrous.

The difference between genius and stupidity is that genius has limits."

Anonymous

Science is a first rate piece of furniture for man's upper chamber, if he has common sense on the ground floor.

Oliver Wendell Holmes

You can't build a reputation on what you're going to do.

Henry Ford

Name the greatest of all inventors: Accident.

Mark Twain

Ideas are like rabbits. You get a couple and learn how to handle them and pretty soon you have a dozen.

Some people see more in a walk around the block than others see in a trip around the world.

A hard fall means a high bounce if you are made of the right material.

Anonymous

You are not what you think you are but, what you think, you are.

Shirley McLain

If the enemy is within range, so are you.

Murphy's Laws of
Combat Operations

Life is like being on a dog sled team.
If you ain't the lead dog, the scenery never changes.

Anonymous

You can't always depend on expert opinion. A turkey, if you ask the turkey, should be stuffed with grasshoppers, grit, and worms.

Anonymous

It's a question of whether we're going forward into the future or past to the back.

Dan Qualye

An idea that is not dangerous is unworthy of being called an idea at all.

Elbert Hubbard

The next time your mind wanders, follow it around for a while.

Lindsay Collier

Orville Wright didn't have a pilot's license.

Gordon MacKenzie

Another word for creativity is courage.

George Prince

29

We can't leave haphazard to chance.

N.F. Simpson

*The things we fear most in organizations -
fluctuations, disturbances, imbalances - are the
primary sources of creativity.*

Margaret Wheatley

*Bring ideas in and entertain them royally, for one
of them may be king.*

Mark Van Doren

What soap is to the body, laughter is to the soul.

Yiddish proverb

*I don't paint things. I only paint the difference
between things.*

Henri Matisse

The silly question is the first intimation of some totally new development.

Alfred North Whithead

Opportunities always exist for the person who can think unconventionally.

George Eastman

Thunder is good. Thunder is impressive. But it's the lightning that does the work.

Mark Twain

The time you enjoy wasting is not wasted time.

Bertrand Russell

Nobody realizes that some people expend tremendous energy merely to be normal.

Al Camus

31

If in the last few years you haven't discarded a major opinion or acquired a new one then check your pulse, you may be dead.

Gelett Burgess

Change is like a steam roller. If you are not on the steamroller, there's a real good chance you might become part of the road.

Marvin Cetron

The road to success is always under construction.

Anonymous

Everything of importance has been seen by someone who did not discover it.

Alfred North Whitehead

Creativity is a type of learning process where the teacher and pupil are located in the same individual.

Arthur Koestler

Things will get better - despite our efforts to improve them.

Will Rogers

The trouble with the future is that it usually arrives before we're ready for it.

Arnold Glasow

Not everything that matters can be measured, and not everything that can be measured matters.

Albert Einstein

Where there's a will there's a won't."

Where there's a will there's at least 43 relatives."

Anonymous

One can never consent to creep when one feels an impulse to soar."

Helen Keller

It takes courage to be creative. Just as soon as you have a new idea, you are a minority of one.

Paul Torrence

You've removed most of the roadblocks to success when you've learned the difference between motion and direction.

Bill Copeland

Great spirits have always encountered violent opposition from mediocre minds.

Albert Einstein

A hen is only an egg's way of making another egg.

Samuel Butler

Whether you believe you can or believe you can't, you're absolutely right.

I'm looking for a lot of men who have an infinite capacity to know what can't be done.

Henry Ford

The more you know, the more you know you don't know.

Aristotle

It takes a long time to grow young.

Picasso

We don't know who discovered water, but we're pretty sure it wasn't a fish.

J. Bruce Francis

Things may come to those who wait, but only the things left by those who hustle.

Abraham Lincoln

Good ideas, like good pickles, are crisp, enduring, and devilishly hard to make.

Rushworth Kidder

When your heart speaks take good notes.

Life is too short to wear tight shoes.

Yurok Indian proverbs

*Every right idea, no matter how good it is, is
eventually the wrong idea.*

Peter Drucker

*If I give you a dollar and you give me a dollar
we each have a dollar. If I give you an idea and
you give me an idea, we each have two ideas.*

Anonymous

*More than any time in history mankind faces a
crossroads. One path leads to despair and utter
hopelessness, the other to total extinction. Let us
pray we have the wisdom to choose correctly.*

Woody Allen

37

The awful thing is that you can never be aware of what you are not aware of.

Edward DeBono

Conception is easier than birth - and a good deal more pleasant too.

Anonymous

So long as there's a bit of laugh going on, things are all right. As soon as this infernal seriousness, like a greasy sea, heaves up, everything is lost.

D.H. Lawrence

Never go to a doctor whose office plants have died.

Erma Bombeck

Success is going from failure to failure with great enthusiasm.

Winston Churchill

I skate to where the puck is going to be, not to where it is.

Wayne Gretsky

Where there is an open mind there will always be a frontier.

Charles Kettering

If you lose the power to laugh, you lose the power to think.

Clarence Darrow

If I have ever made valuable discoveries, it has been owing more to patient attention than to any other talent.

Isaac Newton

The life of a creative person is lead, directed, and controlled by boredom. Avoiding boredom is one of our most important purposes.

Saul Stoppard

The winner sees a green near every sand trap. The loser sees a sand trap near every green.

Anonymous

One who offers an insult writes it in sand, but for the one who receives it, it's chiseled in bronze.

Giovanni Guareschi

40

It takes both rain and sunshine to make a rainbow.

Imagination is only intelligence having fun.

Anonymous

The ability to relate and to connect, sometimes in odd and yet striking fashion, lies at the very heart of any creative use of the mind, no matter in what field or discipline.

George J. Seidel

It's better to build a fence at the top of the cliff than a hospital at the bottom.

Ann Landers

The best way to predict the future is to invent it.

Alan Kay

People do not quit playing because they grow old, they grow old because they quit playing.

Oliver Wendell Holmes

If anything goes bad, I did it. If anything goes semi-good, then we did it. If anything goes real good, then you did it. That's all it takes to get people to win football games for you.

Bear Bryant

Everywhere you trip is where the treasure lies.

Warren Bennis

The future of the future is the present.

Marshal McLuen

*Only those who risk going too far can know how
far one can go.*

T. S. Eliot

*If you don't change your direction you'll likely end
up where you're going.*

Chinese proverb

*Anyone who thinks they are indispensable should
stick their finger in a bowl of water and notice the
hole it leaves when it's pulled out.*

Harvey Mackay

Creativity is the sudden succession of stupidity.

Edwin Land

I like nonsense. It wakes up the brain cells.
Fantasy is a necessary ingredient in living.

Dr. Seuss

Nothing encourages creativity like the chance to
fall on one's face.

James Finley

Many ideas grow better when transplanted into
another mind than in the one they sprang up.

Oliver Wendell Holmes

Small opportunities are often the beginning of
great enterprises.

Demosthenes

Beaten paths are for beaten men.

Eric Johnston

Two roads diverged in the wood and I took the one less traveled by, and that has made all the difference.

Robert Frost

Every man takes the limits of his own field of vision for the limits of the world.

Arthur Schopenhauer

Never underestimate the relative unimportance of everything.

Steve Allen Jr.

It's always more fun to do the impossible because that's where there is less competition.

Walt Disney

Stressed is just desserts spelled backwards.

Marianna Nunes

All men and women are created creative. We were all children once.

Sidney Shore

You can't think about thinking unless you think about thinking about something.

Seymour Papert

Common sense is just a collection of prejudices acquired by age 18.

Albert Einstien

Projects are never completed. You only find a temporary place to pause.

Wujec's Maxim

There are two kinds of people. Those who finish what they start and so on....

Robert Byrne

A hunch is your creativity trying to tell you something.

Frank Capra

The illiterate of the 21st century will not be those who cannot read or write, but those who cannot learn, unlearn, and relearn.

Alvin Toffler

A hunch is creativity trying to tell you something.

Frank Capra

The only two things that are infinite are the universe and human stupidity, and I'm not sure about the former.

Albert Einstien

History celebrates few persons who waited for inspiration.

Ned Arthur

Whenever man comes up with a better mousetrap, nature immediately comes up with a better mouse.

James Carswell

The whole difference between construction and creation is exactly this: that a thing constructed can be loved after it is constructed; but a thing created is loved before it exists.

Charles Dickens.

The definition of a lousy product is one that has no enemies within the company.

Arno Penzias

Sometimes trying to tune up an old engine is like putting lipstick on a pig.

Ross Perot

When one door closes, another one opens somewhere.

Yorok Indian proverb

The creation of a thousand forests is in one acorn.

Ralph Waldo Emerson

I couldn't wait for success so I went ahead without it.

Jonathan Winters

Think of the trouble the world would save if it paid more attention to nonsense.

E.B. White

Nothing would be done at all if a man waited until he could do it so well that no one could find fault with it.

Cardinal Newman

Making the simple complicated is commonplace; making the complicated simple, awesomely simple, that's creativity.

Charles Mingus

The only people with whom you should try to get even with are those who have helped you.

Mae Maloo

The problem with creativity is not how to get new, innovative thoughts into your mind, but how to get old ones out. Every mind is a room packed with archaic furniture. You must get the old furniture of what you know, think, and believe out before anything new can get in. Make empty space in any corner of your mind and creativity will instantly fill it.

Dee Hock

Hiding your head in the sand isn't the best way to hold your head up.

Anonymous

Persistence is the hard work that you do after you are tired of doing the hard work you already did.

Newt Gingrich

Anyone who sees a psychiatrist ought to have his head examined.

A verbal contract isn't worth the paper it's written on.

Samuel Goldwyn

Creative minds are rarely tidy.

Creativity can be described as letting go of certainties.

Creativity in science could be described as the act of putting two and two together to make five.

Creativity is the ability to introduce order into the randomness of nature.

Anonymous

Beware of the turtle. It makes progress only when it sticks its neck out.

Anonymous

Always look out for number one. But don't step on number two.

Rodney Dangerfield

It's better to have people in a tent looking out than to have them outside the tent looking in.

Lyndon Johnson

If we know what we're doing, it isn't innovation.

Elaine Hazen

53

The more you think, the more time you have.

Henry Ford

Laughter is like changing a baby's diaper. It doesn't permanently solve any problems, but it makes things more acceptable for a while.

Anonymous

There are hundreds of uses for cowhide, but the most important one is to hold the cow together.

Texas Bix Bender

Better to remain silent and be thought a fool than to speak up and remove all doubt.

Abraham Lincoln

If there's no juice in the orange then stop squeezing it.

Den Black

Being in outer space helped me to discover my inner space.

Edgar Mitchell – astronaut

Without long, lovely moments spent in daydreams, life becomes an iron-ribbed sterile puffing machine.

C.N. Parkinson

Life is like a box of chocolates.

Learn the infield fly rule. This will give you a good perspective on life.

Forest Gump

If you find a road with no obstacles, chances are it won't lead anywhere.

Anonymous

Not everything counts that can be counted, and not everything that can be counted counts.

Albert Einstein

The certainty of misery is better than the misery of uncertainty.

Pogo

It don't mean a thing if it ain't got that swing.

Duke Ellington

Organizations are like fish. They begin to stink from the head down.

Moe Stein

Creativity is the ability to see relationships where none exist.

Anonymous

If you aren't fired with enthusiasm, you'll be fired with enthusiasm.

Vince Lombardi

A long habit of not thinking a thing wrong gives it a superficial appearance of being right.

Thomas Paine

You are only as good as you dare to be bad.

Timothy Hutton

Any useful statement about the future should seem ridiculous now.

Hawaii Research Center
for Future Studies

A river is like intelligence. The deeper it is, the less noise it makes.

Anonymous

*You can really see a lot by observing.
If you see a fork in the road, take it.*

Yogi Berra

A person needs a little madness, or else they never dare cut the rope and be free.

Nikos Kazantzakis

I never know how much of what I say is true.

Bette Midler

I was going to buy a copy of The Power of Positive Thinking and then thought, "What good would that do?

Ronnie Shakes

Our problems are mostly behind us. What we have to do now is fight the solutions.

Chicago Tribune

Big shots are only little shots who keep on shooting.

A diamond is just a piece of coal that stuck to the job.

Anonymous

It's much easier to ride a horse in the direction it's going.

Allen Klein

In creating, the only hard thing's to begin; A grass blade is no easier to make than an oak.

James Russell Lowell

The bridges you cross before you come to them are usually over rivers that aren't there.

Anonymous

The secret to creativity is knowing how to hide your sources.

Albert Einstein

If two people on the same job agree all the time then one is useless. If they disagree all the time, then both are useless.

Daryl F. Zanuck

If at first you don't succeed, try, try again. Then give up. There's no sense being a damn fool about it.

W.C. Fields

If it works, it's obsolete.

One person's sacred cow is another person's Big Mac.

Anonymous

Nothing is less productive than to make more efficient what should not be done at all.

Peter Drucker

You will become as small as your controlling desire, as great as your dominant aspiration.

James Allen

You will always underestimate the future.

Charles F. Kettering

Smile, it improves your face value.

Anonymous

Imagination grows by exercise and, contrary to popular belief, is more powerful in the mature than the young.

W. Somerset Maugham

In spite of the cost of living, it's still popular.

Do not take life too seriously. You'll never get out of it alive.

Anonymous

When you talk you can only say something you know. When you listen, you may learn what someone else knows.

Anonymous

To gain knowledge, add something everyday. To gain wisdom, get rid of something every day.

Lao Tzu

Knowledge is power, but only wisdom is liberty.

Will Durant

Successful companies make short term profits for a long time.

Anonymous

The notes I handle no better than many pianists. But the pauses between the notes - ah, that is where the art resides.

Artur Schnabel

An invention is like the punch line of a joke - completely logical and completely unexpected.

Jake Rabinow

Research is what I'm doing when I don't know what I'm doing.

Werner Von Braun

The sooner you fall behind, the more time you'll have to catch up.

Stenderup

No great idea ever entered the mind through the mouth.

Anonymous

*Once you have taken the impossible
into your calculations, its possibilities
become potentially limitless.*

Anonymous

To know what to ask is already to know half.

Aristotle

*You can keep the organization vital by not taking
the organization too seriously.*

3M CEO

*Choose a job you love and you'll never have to
work another day in your life.*

Confusus

*The greatest opportunity for growth lies in
overcoming things you are afraid of.*

Brooke Knapp

Expecting the world to be fair to you because you are good is like expecting the bull not to charge you because you are a vegetarian.

Harold Kushner

People who are always raising the roof usually don't have much in the attic.

Anonymous

Problems are only opportunities with thorns in them.

Hugh Miller

The world we have made as a result of the level of thinking we have done thus far creates problems that we cannot solve at the same level at which we created them.

Albert Einstein

*If you look for the best in people it will keep you
so busy you won't find time to notice the worst.*

Anonymous

*A great way to find out what you want from life is
to write your own epitaph.*

Libbie Fudim

It is difficult to predict, especially about the future.

Peter Drucker

*Good judgment comes from experience and
experience comes from bad judgment.*

Tom Watson

Success is a journey, not a destination.

A rut is a grave with the ends knocked out.

Anonymous

The search for happiness is one of the chief sources of unhappiness.

Eric Hoffer

When you make up your mind, your mind stops making.

Stein X. Leikanger

I am not young enough to know everything.

Little Zen Companion

Progress might have been all right once, but it has gone on too long.

Ogden Nash

The trophies on one's shelf do not win tomorrow's games.

Buck Rogers

On spaceship earth there are no passengers - only crew.

Buckminster Fuller

You usually don't drown in the sea, you drown in a puddle.

Anonymous

Creativity is not a major issue in Japan. No, it's the only issue.

Hiro Takeuchi

I know God won't give me anything I can't handle. I just wish he wouldn't trust me so much.

Mother Teresa

Innovation is easy. You simply create the exact opposite of everything people wanted the day before.

Toshiba add

The enemy diversion you are ignoring is the main attack.

Friendly fire – isn't.

Murphy's Laws of Combat Operations

Inspiration could be called inhaling the memory of an act never experienced.

Ned Rorem

Every day we spend without learning something is a day lost.

Beethoven

If something is worth doing, it's worth doing wrong at least the first time.

Anonymous

Anyone who can spell a word only one way is an idiot.

W. C. Fields

To create, first you must destroy.

Picasso

An optimist sees an opportunity in every calamity; a pessimist sees a calamity in every opportunity.

Anonymous

How do you find the line between practical and essential, especially when practical is so essential?

Harlan Cleveland

Luck is what happens when preparation and opportunity meet.

Horge Hagedorn

I'll give you a definite maybe.

Samuel Goldwyn

A great many people think they are thinking when they are merely rearranging their prejudices.

William James

Don't accept your dog's admiration as conclusive evidence that you are wonderful.

Ann Landers

*It is the supreme art of the teacher to awaken joy
in creative expression and knowledge.*

Albert Einstein

*One sees great things from the valley, only small
things from the peak.*

G. K. Chesterson

*In the beginner's mind there are many
possibilities. In the expert's mind there are only a
few.*
Suzuki

*Average is like having one foot in ice water and
one foot in scalding water. On the average you're
comfortable.*

*Yesterday is a canceled check; tomorrow is a
promissory note; today is cash. Spend it wisely.*

Anonymous

People who complain about the way the ball bounces are usually the ones who dropped it.

Anonymous

A fanatic is a person who, upon losing his perspective, redoubles his effort.

R. E. Pigman

Once a new technology runs over you, you are not part of the steam roller; you are part of the road.

MIT Media Lab

Be kind to your friends. Without them you'd be a total stranger.

Anonymous

If you torture data sufficiently it will confess to anything.

Fred Menger

By staying at the rear of the advance, you can be at the forefront of the retreat.

Anonymous

Horse sense is what keeps horses from betting on what people do.

Oscar Wilde

The more you appreciate yourself, the more you will appreciate.

Swami Beyondana

Swallow your pride occasionally. It's nonfattening.

Frank Tyger

One way to get high blood pressure is to go climbing over molehills.

Anonymous

*Some people never hear opportunity knock
because they are too busy knocking opportunity.*

Hal Chadwick

*Any significantly advanced technology is
indistinguishable from magic.*

Anonymous

*It is only when we develop others that we
permanently succeed.*

Harvey Firestone

*If you have always done it that way, it is probably
wrong.*

Charles Kettering

There is no breakthrough without breakage

Norman Brown

If the parts don't fit the theory then change the theory.

Albert Einstein

If everyone is thinking alike, then no one is thinking.

General George Patton

Only intuition can protect you from the most dangerous individual of all, the articulate incompetent.

Robert Bernstein

Teamwork is essential. It gives the enemy some other people to shoot at.

Murphy's Laws of Combat Operations

There are two ways to find a breakthrough: Play the rules better than anybody else; Break the rules better than anybody else.

Bob Hacker

Luck is the residue of design.

Branch Rickey

In times of rapid change experience may be your own worst enemy.

J. Paul Getty

Reality is for people who lack imagination.

I shall never respect my brains until I pick a few gold coins from them.

Thomas Wolfe

Your worst humiliation is only someone else's momentary entertainment.

Karen Crocket

What most of us need is more horsepower and less exhaust.

Anonymous

No matter how many friends you have, the best predictor of how many people will show up for your funeral is the weather that day.

Anonymous

The quality of an organization can never exceed the quality of the minds that make it up.

Harold R. McAlindon

Learn the current rules so you'll know when you're violating them.

John Fleider

Speak softly and sweetly. That way your words won't be so hard to swallow when you have to eat them.

Anonymous

We judge ourselves by what we feel capable of doing. Others judge us by what we've already done.

Henry Longfellow

Japanese companies win not because they have smarter managers but because they have developed ways to harness the wisdom of an anthill.

C. K. Gary

Everything should be made as simple as possible, but not simpler.

Albert Einstein

The advice your son rejected is now being given to your grandson.

Anonymous

Coincidence is God's way of remaining anonymous.

Anonymous

Be obscure clearly.

E.B. White

A ship in the harbor is safe. But that's not what ships are for.

John Shedd

It usually takes me about 3 weeks to prepare a good impromptu speech.

Mark Twain

It is impossible to concentrate on the opposite of an idea.

Anonymous

What great thing would you attempt if you knew you could not fail?

Robert Schuler

Eighty percent of all people consider themselves above average.

Greld

Keep your face to the sun and the shadows will fall behind you.

Texas Bix Bender

If the earth had waited for a precedent, it never would have turned on its axis.

Maria Mitchell, astronomer

Nothing's ever so bad that it can't get worse.

Gattuso

Time is a great teacher. Unfortunately, it kills all its pupils.

Hector Berlioz

Out of confusion comes chaos. Out of chaos comes anarchy and fear. Then comes lunch.

Anonymous

The greatest enemy of any one of our truths may be the rest of the truths.

William Jam

You may not realize it when it happens, but a kick in the teeth may be the best thing in the world for you.

Walt Disney

You can't leave haphazard to chance.

N.F. Simpson

One doesn't discover new lands without consenting to lose sight of the shore for a very long time.

Andre Gide

The future is not only about change, it's about continuity.

David Zach

If you're not confused by what's going on today,
you're just not thinking clearly.

Mrs. Tom Peters

Beware the craftsman who claims twenty years of
experience. It's often just one year of experience
over and over again twenty times.

Anonymous

Lost causes are the
only ones worth fighting for.

Mr. Smith Goes to Washington

The obscure we see eventually, the completely
apparent takes longer.

Edward R. Murrow

85

To gain knowledge add something every day. To gain wisdom, get rid of something every day.

Lao Tzu

The principle obstacle between a man and where he wants to be is himself.

Russel Ackoff

Everything I know is a result of my ignorance.

Anonymous

You don't have to change because survival is not mandatory.

Edward Deming

Live your life at the intersections, not on the highway.

Peter Block

When you're in a hole the first thing you should do is stop digging.

Anonymous

The opposite of a truth is not necessarily a falsehood. It is often an even greater truth.

Neils Bohr

I don't want to achieve immortality through my work. I want to achieve it through not dying.

Woody Allen

As you go through life you are going to have many opportunities to keep your mouth shut. Take advantage of all of them.

James Dent

If you reach your hand into a pool of water with a tight fist, your hand comes up empty. If you reach in with an open fist your hand can catch water.

Wayne Dyer

Freedom is the length of the chain between imagination and reality.

Native American Saying

A new idea is often the result of two old ideas meeting for the first time.

American Electric Power add

Repeatedly curing a system that can cure itself will eventually create a system that can't.

Anonymous

If you use the same recipe you'll get the same bread.

It's difficult to follow the footsteps of someone who leaves no impression.

Anonymous

The key to creativity is yanking convention inside out.

Sony ad

Something hit me very hard once, thinking about what one little man could do. Think of the Queen Elizabeth. The whole ship goes by and then comes the rudder. And there's a tiny thing on the edge of the rudder called a trim tab. It's a miniature rudder. Just moving that little trim tab builds a low pressure that pulls the rudder around. It takes almost no effort at all. So I said that the individual can be a trim tab. Society thinks it's going right by you, and that it's left you altogether. But if you're doing dynamic things mentally, the fact is that you can just put your foot out like that and the whole

89

ship of state is going to turn around

Buckminster (Bucky) Fuller

Genius is nothing more than childhood recovered at will.

Charles Baudelaire

Don't worry about people stealing your ideas. If your ideas are any good you'll have to ram them down people's throats.

Howard Aiken

Failure is permissible just as long as it's only temporary. The one time you don't want to fail is the last time you try.

Kettering

Dare to be naïve.

R Buckminster Fuller

*Failure is just part of the culture of innovation.
Accept it and become stronger.*

Albert Yu

*There ain't no rules around here. We're trying to
accomplish something.*

Thomas Edison

*Clear out a corner of your mind and creativity will
instantly fill it.*

Dee Hock

Creative minds are rarely tidy.

Anonymous

Creativity can be described as letting go of certainties.

Gail Sheehy

Creativity in science could be described as the act of putting two and two together to make five.

Arthur Koestler

Creativity is a lot like looking at the world through a kaleidoscope. You look at a set of elements, the same ones everyone sees, but then reassemble those floating bits into an enticing new possibility.

Rosabeth Moss Kanter

Creativity is the ability to introduce order into the randomness of nature.

Eric Hoffer

I like nonsense; it wakes up the brain cells.
Fantasy is a necessary ingredient in living.

Dr Seuss

Making the simple complicated is commonplace;
making the complicated simple, awesomely simple,
that's creativity.

Charles Mingus

Nothing encourages creativity like the chance to
fall flat on one's face.

James Finley

In every work of genius we recognize our own
rejected thoughts. They come back to us with a
certain alienated majesty.

Ralph Waldo Emerson

Innovation is fostered by information gathered from new connections; from insights gained by journeys into other disciplines or places.

Margaret J. Wheatley

The best way to have a good idea is to have a lot of ideas.

Linus Pauling

Allow for the inherent sloppiness of innovation.

Tom Peters

The innovation point is the pivotal moment when talented and motivated people seek the opportunity to act on their ideas and dreams.

W. Arthur Porter

An inventor is simply a person who doesn't take his education too seriously. You see, from the time a person is six years old until he graduates from college he has to take three or four examinations a year. If he flunks once, he is out. But an inventor is almost always failing. He tries and fails maybe a thousand times. If he succeeds once then he's in. These two things are diametrically opposite. We often say that the biggest job we have is to teach a newly hired employee how to fail intelligently. We have to train him to experiment over and over and to keep on trying and failing until he learns what will work.

Charles Kettering

The more original a discovery, the more obvious it seems afterwards.

Arthur Koestler

95

In the following quotes I have either lost or never had the originator. My apologies for that and, if you are the source, I will you my first born great, great grandchild.

Success comes in cans. Failure in cants.

Never be afraid to try something new. Remember, amateurs built the ark. Professionals built the Titanic.

If you can't see the bright side of life, polish the dull side.

How things look on the outside of us depends on how the things are on the inside.

When your dreams turn to dust, vacuum.

The best angle from which to approach any problem is the try-angle.

I've learned that a smile is an inexpensive way to improve your looks.

The greatest pleasure in life is doing what people say you cannot do.

Laughter is the shock absorber that eases the blows of life.

The road to success is dotted with many tempting parking spaces.

Change is the essence of life. Be willing to surrender what you are for what you could become.

To reach a great height a person needs to have great depth.

A half-baked idea is okay as long as it's in the oven.

Promise only what you can deliver, then deliver more than you promise.

People who wait for changes to occur on the outside before they commit to making changes on the inside will never make any changes at all.

Thinkers think and doers do. But until the thinkers do and the doers think, progress will be just another word in the already overburdened vocabulary of talkers who talk.

The only way to see a rainbow is through the rain.

Never think the sky is the limit when there are footprints on the moon.

Opportunities are often missed because we are broadcasting when we should be listening.

Always be flexible. That way you don't get bent out of shape.

Those who bring sunshine into the lives of others cannot keep it from themselves.

Reach for the high apples first. You can get the low ones anytime.

Some people grin and bear it. Others smile and change it.

Some people see more in a walk around the block than others see in a trip around the world.

A hard fall means a high bounce if you are made of the right material.

Well, I hope you enjoyed these quotations. If you are anything like me, you sat down and went through these fairly quickly and are ready to set this book aside. Don't do it! At the very least make it your bathroom reader!

Get these to work for you by going back to the operating manual in the front of the book and forcing yourself to use them in some of the ways suggested. Or make up your own ways of using them. There isn't a quotation in this book that doesn't have the power to influence the way you and your friends and associates think. Let them challenge you to open up your minds and change the way you think. Have fun with them.

I'd love to hear stories about how you were able to use them and I'd also like to know your favorite quotations. My address follows and I look forward to talking with you.

Lindsay Collier
The Villages, Florida
lindsaycollier@comcast.net

About the Author

Lindsay Collier presently resides in The Villages, Florida with his wife, Jean. After serving as a Captain in the US Army Corps of Engineers he joined Eastman Kodak as an engineer and took an early retirement after 25 years. During his tenure at Kodak he became their expert in creative thinking and innovation and went on to become an author, speaker and consultant after his retirement. He has shared his ideas with many organizations in the US and abroad in the form of books, workshops, and keynote presentations.

He'd love to hear from you if you have other quotes to share and can be contacted at <u>lindsaycollier@comcast.net</u>.

Other books by Lindsay Collier

Organizational Mental Floss; How to Squeeze Your
Organization's Thinking Juices

Surviving the Loss of Your Loved One; Jan's Rainbow

How to Live Happily Ever After; 12 Things You Can Do To
Live Forever

Organizational Braindroppings: Musings on Organizational
Breakthrough and Change

The Whack-A-Mole Theory; Creating Breakthrough and
Transformation in Organizations

Get Out of Your Thinking Box; 365 Ways to Brighten Your Life
and Enhance Your Creativity

Jan's Rainbow; Stories of Hope; How Those You Have Loved
and Lost Stay in Touch With You.

See all of Lindsay's books at his Amazon author site.

Amazon.com/author/lindsaycollier